ALSO BY OWEN LEWIS:

poetry

March in San Miguel
Sometimes Full of Daylight
Best Man

poetry/multi-media

New Pictures at an Exhibitio
(with Seymour Bernstein)

essays

Psychotherapies with Children:
Adapting the Psychodynamic Process
(with Jack O'Brien, Dan Pilowsky)

MARRIAGE MAP

poems by
OWEN LEWIS

To Rose and Koen

[signature]

DOS MADRES

2017

DOS MADRES PRESS, INC.
P.O.Box 294, Loveland, Ohio 45140
www.dosmadres.com   editor@dosmadres.com

Dos Madres is dedicated to the belief that the small press is essential
to the vitality of contemporary literature as a carrier of the new voice,
as well as the older, sometimes forgotten voices of the past. And in an
ever more virtual world, to the creation of fine books pleasing to the
eye and hand.

Dos Madres is named in honor of Vera Murphy and Libbie Hughes,
the "Dos Madres" whose contributions have made this press possible.

Dos Madres Press, Inc. is an Ohio Not For Profit Corporation and a
501(c)(3) qualified public charity. Contributions are tax deductible.

Executive Editor: Robert J. Murphy

Illustration & Book Design: Elizabeth H. Murphy
www.illusionstudios.net

Typset in Adobe Garamond Pro, Colonna & Adobe Myungjo
ISBN 978-1-939929-72-3
Library of Congress Control Number: 2016961838

First Edition

ACKNOWLEDGEMENTS

To Ed Hirsch, Martha Rhodes, and Fran Quinn, thankful gratitude for careful reading, insightful responses, invaluable suggestions, and in addition, to Fran, for his help in shaping this volume. To my publisher Robert Murphy, and book designer Elizabeth Murphy for making beautiful books happen.

To my friends who have been available and ready to read and respond: Kate Daniels, Myra Shapiro, Laure-Anne Bosselaar, Geraldine Clarkson, Jim Tolan, Greg Egan, and Boris Thomas.

And to Susan Ennis, inspiration for this book.

*

Special thanks to the journals and their editors where the following poems first appeared, sometimes in earlier versions:

"Bouquet"; *Inch*, winter 2015

"Cut"; *The Adirondack Review,* March, 2011 (as "To the party of the first . . .")

"Please Finish the Conversation"; *Mississippi Review,* summer 2014 (Finalist, 2014 M. R. Contest)

"To My Firstborn"; *London School of Jewish Studies Newsletter,* Dec 21, 2013 (Honorable Mention, 2013 L.S.J.S Contest)

"What Will Happen in the End"; *Connecticut River Review*, summer 2015 (Third Place, 2014 C.R.R. Contest)

"Your Patience: A Prologue"; a selection for The Ver Prize 2015 Anthology (as "Patience")

"Urgency"; *Mom Egg Review*, vol. 14, April 2016

"Fire in the Piano Warehouse"; *Folio 70, Kent and Sussex Poetry Society* 2016 (Second Place, Kent and Sussex Open Poetry Competition)

The poems of the third section first appeared among those in the chapbook "Best Man," *Dos Madres Press*, September 2015. (winner of the 2016 Jean Pedrick Chapbook Prize, New England Poetry Club).

Front Cover: "Path of the Ancients" is used by permission of the artist Karen Davis.

Author photo: Susan Ennis

For Susan,
this map, this guide, these explanations,
with love . . .

The owl had the ability to light up
Athena's blind side, enabling her
to speak the whole truth.

There is nothing more admirable
than when two people who see eye to eye
keep house as a couple, confounding
their enemies and delighting their friends.
—Homer, The Odyssey

TABLE OF CONTENTS

iv. Owl Flight

v. First Waltz

Invocation
Ceremony
Celebration

i.

Plan B

The day I met you

a crane fell, smashing cars, slicing six
stories of corners off a building,
some injuries from the flying debris;

the day I met you the sky opened,
a steel hook descended cloud to street
and as I look back I can see the line,

the fall separating all that came before
and all that would come after. You phoned,
"Streets blocked with crowds, the press,

if you can't get down to the Bowery,
I've got a Plan B . . ."
For a moment without breath—Plan B? . . .

Already you were holding my breath.
My marriage botched, collapsing. Who
had ever considered for me a "Plan B"?

Two Dreams

1.

Tonight—a grandfather clock rowing through a sky wanting to be a sea,
    still wanting to be air.
For a minute I'm a goat playing rhapsodies for you on a violin, and it lasts
    only a minute.
You perch on my shoulder, take the reins of my beard. I'm an angel
    spanning the horizon like the sunrise,
cradling the clock that is singing a lullaby. And now, for a minute,
    you wear a white lace gown!
My head is a chicken's, my beak a clarinet. A cello stands up, plays itself
    weeping.
I straddle your shoulders, holding my whole family in a clutch of balloons
    I let go of.
I'm Moses making up vows, making up minute commandments. A minute
    on wings
above the Friday candles, the lips of God above the cup. The white owl
    flies beyond the moon

into the chandelier that hangs from heaven.

2.

Night—a drifting barge, the paunched pile of my cargo the dross,
   the ash of a furnace long cold.
I am rowing through a heavy sky that is moist like the sea,
   paddling with long outstretched arms
the oily swells, a flotilla of jettisoned possessions—books, chairs,
   a piano keyboard, a coat,
a dried bouquet, pictures, and out of every frame an arm elbowing
   into the dark.
Where are you? Our palms brush, our fingers touch. No words
   from your lips
to say goodbye—*See you in September?* Is this a season of outer space,
   or inner space,
this vacuum where sound is an energy point oscillating on a dark screen,
   a trajectory,
something living light years away? Your hair, miles and miles of dark
   kelp beds, the nets of the sea.

And the barge still drifting.

Broadway and 8th

Months now after we met,
at the edge of the curb
above Broadway's rush and traffic flow—

I'm thinking of my father again,
on the banks of a lake, a fishing trip
I barely tolerated. It was Rideau Lake

in Ontario, an unappreciative teen,
a father who tried, though not overly.
(Even then I knew how mistaken I was.)

Not just my failure to understand
the power of the wrist-flick, the worm-wick,
my feet thumping the boat bottom

breaking reflection, sending ripples
into the late Spring calm as we drifted
under a fallen bough where dragonflies

sunned, numerous as new leaves.
The light has changed many times . . .
I'm jostled by many elbows at Broadway

and 8th. I just left your building . . .
what of this low-flying gull, whimpering
regret that seeps into all the currents,

my father telling the guys about the one I
let go, walleye or bass, my hands
would've stung with its desperate

4

and colorful flipping, this final struggle
a reward for patience, still requiring patience—
there was something worth waiting for—

and that's what I'm trying to figure out
to tell you, mayflies swarming,
not knowing the who I am—never have—

but hoping that the one you caught
I can be, grow in your love and lost
worth. Pull hard on the line,

scoop me into the net. I will try
not to get away. Your hook in my cheek,
it is you will hold me—the you and I

we can know. Help me with patience.
There's much, I have to tell you.
Much I don't understand.

I will

ask to marry you
because when we sleep
I know by thigh, or chest,
you are there, by the wave
of your hand across my back.

Night's trapdoor
opens, the body at the brim
gives its twitch, its fall,
and by the lightest touch
we've got hold

of each other. We've got hold.

ii.

Last Words of a Divorce, Can You Listen?

Your Patience: A Prologue

It still surprises you, I know,
my darting from bed before sunrise.
You're just settling into your deepest sleep;

sleeping night after night together
by now it's set, we'll keep our hours
like the clocks of New York and Paris.

The morning heat cranks the radiators,
and in our bed, in dream's half-slumber,
i-phone near, you're tracking the day's weather,

snow seen as flakes falling
deep within the hand-held screen;
the map shows it started downtown

moving north, and reaching 101st Street,
you text: look out the window. Your eye
on the heavens, your ear listening closely—

I move room to room, reading out loud,
juggling laundry, cats and writing-pads,
cursing the splash of coffee on the rug.

When

she and I raised a brimming chalice
and why did we continue to kiss,
the wine was a rushing current,
an undertow to the whirlpool

of fins and tails slapping
the liquid sheets—we fought
for survival, for which child,
as if a car, will we each take—

but in her mouth,
still, a memory of honey, scent
of clover in a field criss-crossed
and trampled.

Kiss

I kissed her
and she had no lips.
They had been kissed away

before I ever knew her.
Mine are withered too, a mark.
My cheeks end at my mouth.

When we kissed, a clashing of teeth.
How many arguments
can be forgotten? I wanted

other kinds of words—in embrace,
under a tent of skin, a knocking
of bones. Was this

the march of the nightly
army? Who goes?
The eye of the clock is blind.

Enough

Who was it last night? What syllables
up from the lake's silt basin, her voice
entering this room, hovering over

the surprised eyeglasses on my bedside table?
Who was it I fumbled to say hello to, the phone
dropping from my sleeping hand each time? Who was it,

scratched up by the lake's bottom where rocks
pack together like ice cubes at the bottom of a tumbler
holding all these years? Why now, *why now?* She no longer

has a face, a name—(though deep in my dresser drawer,
her empty purse, I have it still)—is that what she came for,
or in it maybe—(shall I look?)—banknotes of currencies now

just souvenirs, or wanting directions to a once-favorite bakery—
(that closed decades ago. Students still, she stood outside
till 4:55 when the pastries went on half sale)—come here

hungry as my morning cat come to ask for what? A drink?
Of what? The lake she sprung from not enough to quench thirst,
its fish not enough to fill her belly? I am caught by a line

that leads only to confusion. "Enough." In whose vocabulary?
"Enough?" I say again and again, the word echoing a corridor
of years until I understand the word is emphatically mine—Enough!

Cut

Cut the table in half
cut each of the twelve chairs
in half cut each dish in half and cut
the cups and split the saucers
this is not Solomon's baby half
a teapot for each eleven paintings
in two's half a spatula half a fridge
a stove dissevered half the wall
of shelves and half of one thousand
six hundred and eight books

let's pause . . . a legal dilemma?

the judge may argue
on precedents for the proper
method of the cutting of books
a rip down the spine a surgical
sideways slice making top
and bottom halves or a dissection
of lengthwise portions leaving
a whole story of half paragraphs

so here's a concession

when the houses and all
the chimneys and all the roofs
and all the trees and shrubs
all the rugs and all the drawers
the windows doors and keys
when the bed is finally cut in half

you can have first pick of the piles

and after all the pots the pans
the spoons forks and knives are cut
and there's one knife left
the one that's been doing the cutting

you get the knife

Aftermath

The season of cyclone, ninety mile-per-hour
winds ripping out of mouths frothing with words,
out of nostrils, out of ears. Through the roar

who can listen? A last look at these piles
of possession, what comes with thirty years.
I consign my share to the bulldozer.

Half of the whole is nothing. Is worse.
The nails that held us together pierce our hands,
our feet; the vista of the picture window,

once a living-room's gesture, is glass in shards
of snowfall, a stinging wind and our cheeks
scabbed and pocked. A last look—

What will I keep?
What will she? And if we throw
everything away, everything . . .

I leave her.
I leave her a picture. I leave
a whole lover.

Estate

Swept through the front door
with the group of house-hunters—
    something familiar about that door.
Foyer slate still burnished, unscratched.
Two steps down, the living room,

a clock in about the usual place,
the hands fallen from the center,
crossed, cast down inside the crystal.
By the window a pair of easy chairs,
askew. Photos I expected to recognize.
A pair of lookers, whispering.

The doorbell rings a misplaced tune,
chords of Scheherazade, and dancing.
A girl and her grandmother whirl
the rooms waving scarves and arms.
I follow the trace of them, veering.
The lookers tap walls, test windows.

In the dining room, a packed table.
A seder's going on.
                    Everything's in order.
A twenty-three-year-old, brisket fed
with his bride-to-be, full
of confidence he announces their decision.
What was he expected to know?
    He opens the door for Elijah,

throws their doubts far into the night
and it's a thirty-year arc to its boomerang.

In the kitchen, face-size daisies
are smiling across the wallpaper.
The grandmother hands magic-
markers to her three grandchildren
to graffiti their names to a flower.

Lookers enter the kitchen, compliment
the floor's many piney knots and branches
start to rise up from the floor—at once
many seasons of fir growth and shedding,

an owl hoots, flapping up the stairwell.
A white-tailed deer bucking the hall.
Through a ceiling crack, flying squirrels.

A window breaks and the boomerang
of doubt wings through the glass-
glistening an early snow.

The children, the children
     push through the forest
to the back door. November
when I arrived but out back
July 4th, the lawn sprouting flags,
the kids naked, sprouting wings,
their chins and bellies dripped
with melting blue and red ice-pops.
     I run after them, can't catch them,

ever, any of the moments,
                    can't catch the moment

when the marriage soured, the moment
the grandmother's cells turned bad
and the children now, if I could see
the moments of mistake, For-Sale sign
            swinging in the guts

                    if I buy this house, if I buy it back,
        if I buy this house . . .

The Gett

"One who is not well-versed in the laws of divorce and marriage should not involve himself in such matters. Those who disregard this directive are more destructive than the generation which caused the great flood." (Talmud, Kiddushin 6a)

1.

I am asked to sit at a table across the room.
Two old Rabbis with beards from the mountaintop
and one trim Rabbi from the modern age welcome me
to the *Bet Din.*

There's another table to my right, empty
where she, the ex-, should be, now refusing any room
the two of us. A Jewish joke?—just for my wife,
two divorces!

A kippa I put on, that would be better they say,
hovering over the New York State driver's license ID.
So where's the beard? You looked more . . . They squint at
the picture
looking for a Jew.

Today I am exactly 59½. The half-birthday.
Should I expect half a cake, half a present?
Today I will be delivered half a life. The final separation,
one half from the other.

2.

This is happening
during daylight hours
on the sixteenth day
of the month of Kislev,
five thousand, seven hundred and seventy one years
after the creation of the world.

And this week we read
parsha Va-yeishev: when young Joseph
reached Shechem a man asked him
what he was looking for.
I am looking for my brothers.
Do you know where they are pasturing?

3.

Asher Ben Simcha, known as....
Is it O-wen or Ow-en?
Son of Seymour known as Sy?

When we write it in Hebrew
it is different. We can make
no mistakes. It will not be valid.

What is it my mistakes invalidate?

May we continue?
The Gett is an agreement—a letter
to your wife—

of severance, releasing her to choose
another. Are you sure
you do this with free will?

And what is it that makes will free?
    If I ask, he'll tell me to study Talmud.

4.

Rabbis—

I walked here on my own two feet.
I checked my agenda book three times.
The *Bet Din*, House of the Court.
And across the street your neighbor,
The Fashion Institute of Technology.
I passed four restaurants with foods
of Malaysia, Korea, Ireland and Argentina
where I am sure you have never eaten.

I have no appetite.

5.

We must write this with your instruments
and I will give you as a gift a feather
and a jar of ink. Hold them in the air.
They are yours. Now lend them to me.
The quill and my hand will be your hand,
and not one word will be in error.
This a man can do.

6.

All vows must be released.

Do you recall ever saying to anyone
whosoever that you were feeling forced
and if a whatsoever word was heard
by a whosoever person do you take
back the words because ifsoever
it may be held by a someone-soever passerby
and yes you must say I Asher ben Simcha
known as Ow-en son of Seymour known as Sy
do withdraw the ifsoevers and whatsoevers
from the ears of the whosoevers

for now and eternity?

7.

For now and eternity....

when love has left the feet and left
the sidewalk and marched itself
up above the streetlamps,

up the invisible incline
where pant legs
catch the thermal drifts...

you might see a stretch of scarf
whisk past your window, or a glove,
or a coat thinking itself a kite...

it turns upon itself and there
mid-air inside-out,
it's empty.

8.

The Gett is written
on a sheet of paper or parchment
or hide, not related to anything
that is still attached to the ground—

like a fig leaf
like the side of a tree.

Twelve long lines are etched
into the clean sheet of paper
with two short lines for the witnesses
and stroke by stroke

the letters
fall like wood chips

axed from the trunk of an oak.
The tree has solid girth,
more than middle age
in its long forest life,

and being November
the other trees have dropped their leaves.

Metal cleaves wood
and wood like bone
resists the blows the heavy strokes
the iron wing its steady flight,

a fissure in the low slate sky,
the clang of meeting, the severance

bark from its tree, splinters from wood
silver like sparks. Stroke by black stroke
on the once-unblemished white
the sacrificial calf without a bruise

and there the gimmel and tet
of the rootless word—Gett—

that means nothing, the only two letters
in the family of the Hebrew alphabet
when coupled
            cannot make a real word.

9.

The scribe takes out a crumpled hank
of Kleenex from his deep pocket.

Some of the letters won't dry
as if the ink would rather stay in the pot.

He is a grandfather to eighteen children
and great-grandfather to three.

He has dabbed many eyes and noses
and wiped jam from many little mouths.

He is gentle with his letters.

10.

My scribe,
beause she has absented herself,
you will also be my agent.
This is prescribed.

What words you will speak
will be mine. Your mouth,
my mouth, the shake of your hand
now the shake of mine.

Can I ask you to give her a watch
inscribed many years ago?
I don't know what time it keeps.
And I don't know how to keep time.

If you wind it back you will see
with my eyes a woman to me
once beautiful and you will hear
with my ears a carillon voice.

Can you also see the spill
of water that rinsed the babies' heads
or the bundle of them in white towels
or the hand that long ago clasped mine?

But you will not see her betrayal
because I no longer think about it.
It must be there on the calendars,
somewhere, but I haven't kept them.

And her absence, whenever
it began. It must be there, too,
a mark, a gesture I could have seen.
Your clock, Rabbi, presses on.

Your letter, my letter, won't be mailed.
You'll fold it to a size that will fit
her naked hands free of rings
or bracelets or band-aids

and down it will float
from your hands which are my hands
the way a feather slowly zig-zags
through air, defying gravity

for a moment or two
holding back its arrival into the cup
of her palms pressed together—
show her how to receive it—

and the letter in its moment
of falling, drifts,
a leaf through its seasons,
and you can glimpse a lifetime.

My witnesses, who have watched
many letters falling in the autumn forest
the floor carpeted with yellow and orange
and red and the russet smell of an ending

and the errors of the souls before you
were long accepted before other witnesses
watched them sign their first pledge . . .

my witnesses . . .
make sure she grasps the letter well,
tucks it under her thin arm
and walks with it
a full body-length into her future.

iii.

Cemetery, Cedar Knolls

Post-Script, Unwritten Letter

Taking every memory that came to me like a hand in the dark,
    sometimes leading, sometimes waiting to be led, sometimes grabbing
                                     for your hand to wrestle

the night—or did you find me, brother, reaching between the planes
    of the dark? When you were speaking, I wanted to know from where
                                       what unfolded shadow,

and I made myself get up, scratch ink to paper like the children we were
    digging through the backyard soil, determined to get to China,
                                    the spot under the swings

where our feet whisked the ground before each pendulum soar, and if
    we could rise out of the earth, we'd find our way through it . . .
                                    if I could,

where do we go? We leave the house from the front door, along the walk
    that curves across the lawn. The crimson king maple has just been planted,
                                    a sapling

once staked against the wind, grown wide now giving lots of shade,
    and the stones, as they were without wear, both these
                                    and the marker.

At the end of the driveway, a mailbox, its red flag always up, unwaving.
    Wherever you've been you'll have something to tell me. I expected
                                    to know more.

Introducing

So you'll be there, I'm sure.
Where, how, don't know.
A pea-face in my boutonniere?
Static in my bride's veil?

I've been trying to figure out
how to introduce you.
You didn't like the first wife.
She kept that nose in the air.

This one, you'll like. You will.
So, Jason meet Susan, Susan,
Jason. One day under the *chuppah*
the Rabbi will call: *Yaacov ben Simcha.*

Like the angels—Jacob, son
of Happiness. Come with me.
Everyone, generations, will be
there. You'll ride on my shoulder—

Best Man!

So,

I am still mad at you.
Every week another call

from a pharmacy, a burnt-out Bronx
neighborhood, or Brooklyn.

Vicodin, Dexedrine, shopping lists.
Benzos. That last visit you took

my prescription pad, sold it.
I refused your calls.

From Florida. From the ICU.
Frantic, your girlfriend overdosed.

Our grandmother told me you were ok.
She cooked you a pair of fried eggs.

I've never known how to think
about your end, so, often I just don't.

Hearing Him?

So you think you've called me up?
   I've called on you.
                 The scratch
on your back. The way you must
think
   about me when nostalgia
moves.
     Not so, bubbeleh,
kiddo, hermano mio.
             It's me
digging you out.
                 Interrupting.
         Disrupting.

I can make the fork drop
           from your hand,
the sun glare
     right in your eye,

make your dick shrink
in the middle of oo-
           la-lah love.

I'm a termite in the wood
of your brain. Calling 1-800-
              exterminator.
Calling 911.
       Calling
look at yourself in the mirror.

   I am the shower mist.

Thaw

I hate March—white flowers pushing
the edges, Mother traipsing us
around the yard to see those little blooms,
birthday presents—yours—she called them.

She's gone, too, and who's to celebrate
the scatter of white snowdrops?
They shame me, their strength,
each lifting a plaque of ice. The snow lies,

a smoothing of contours across the yard.
Now, a jagged branch, an elbow sticking through,
a poke in the side it prods what lurks,
what hides within any person's body as if,

from the start, that body's death note
were already written, Mother's cancer,
Father's failing lungs, so it's March 12th
at 7:32 pm, doesn't matter the year, the decade,

again the scatter of white pills across your bed.

En Route

(Beth Israel Cemetery)

It doesn't seem to matter, visiting
or not. Who the hell's here?
So many people left pebbles near
to say hello. Not one for you.

Who's watching, a town
of relatives, on Ridgedale Avenue,
Cedar Knolls. Not my Xanadu.
En route to an aunt who remembers

and friends who don't. Can't
look at your name, staring,
the headline always blaring:
Found After Three Days.

Bellaire Motel, Miami, hundred-degree
nights. The air a fever, coma
oozing from your eyes. No diploma
needed to read this dark. Your face

running off your cheeks, in rivulets.
Back home, the northern earth took hold,
hardened eyes to praise the cold,
and those who cried had ice for tears.

I'm here again, hello?
What muck! No one tending this ground.
After thirty years still sinking down,
as if, only now, inviting a stay.

There's nothing here, or tell me—

Get the fuck away!
                You said—*Get away?*
You really told me to get away?

New Museum

Even some parents wanted to know
what's here: fossil fish and old bones;
amethyst, lava stone and granite;

luna moths, scorpions, and cicadas;
coins from Timbuktu; letters from Russia;
five kinds of oak leaf, blackbird and seagull

feathers, bear-tooth, bear-claw, snake-skin;
formaldehyde frog, dog brain, calf heart.
Three minutes to opening, kid brother

jumps the stairs, trips, collapses a leg
on the display table. Insects crushed,
cicada cracked in several pieces—

I'll be 29 when they next come
out of the earth. Heart and brain
lying next to each other on the floor.

Almost used to him ruining things.
Outside the garage I take down the sign:
Line Forms Here (with an arrow).

I would have let them in two by two,
ready to sail them to new worlds.

At The Devereau School

We were once three kids. *Hey Jude,*
Don't make it bad—driving there, radio noise.
Where do I find him? *Anytime you feel the pain, refrain.*

Bare trees brooming the drive. Welcome?
They send me to the Somebody-Somebody Building.
Inside, a row of army cots stretching back in a warehouse

meant for raising chickens. He's fourteen, hunched on his bed,
back to me. *They're all whack here,* he says, as if I had just come
from the kitchen with a sandwich, roast beef, mayo, provolone.

Medicines making him heavy. He eats because there's nothing
else to do. I'm just out of college. It's dim, with the dark
laundry smell of twenty boys, the overhead fan stirring currents

of neglect. Anyone telling them to change their underwear?
I give him a Grateful Dead sweatshirt, but I'm shivering
and he gives me his black cardigan with his name-tag inside—

I keep it on till the spring. He reaches for a hug, distracted,
fingers the gold amulet on my neck. He's already taken so much
I just give it to him. He'll sell it later, now tucks it inside his shirt,

tilts his head to ask, embarassed what he can't remember—
chai—as numbers meaning eighteen, as letters, life.
                              Hey Jude, don't let me down!

Advice

If you visit someone in jail
you'll leave part of yourself there.
You can't actually give some
thing to the other person like
a pack of lifesavers or a note
from your pocket or some
dollars. There aren't window
bars you can reach through
to shake hands. It's plexiglass
with a circle of little holes so
what you leave has to pass
that barrier. It might be
a look that tries to be kind
but is really a lot of questions
that can't be answered. It's
not a bunch of words because
it's noisy and confused and
everybody else's words mix in.
It will be something from inside
of you like a lungful of air
you've brought from outside.
It could be spring and warm
and full of color or winter
that is crisp and ice-blue. But
when you pass this season on
you'll take a season in
that's full of very mean things
that will fill you up and be in-
side of you and make you think
you should be there too so you
won't think that it's time
to leave until the guard taps

your back because twenty
minutes are over now
that seem like twenty days
and the doors close and you're
outside in the air of the season
you brought inside and what's
in and out or right and wrong
aren't clear and when you stop
at the deli for a coffee and tuna
sandwich you don't know how
you passed a bill to the cashier
or how she passed you change
and why is she smiling or how
your hand could lift the cup
past the barrier or the sandwich
right up to your open mouth.

Gutter Spill

Gutter spill
                    gravel
          under cheek and arm skin
tattoos a picture of night

after clock-stop
the bakery's yeast rises into the dawn

          the sky so hungry it eats its own rising

sun
                    mid-morning visit
to a forty-second street shop
          flowers painted on the walls waist high
                    with holes in each center
                    with sucking mouths on the other side
                    dicks grinding away at the wallflowers

          men adjusting themselves meander away

endless grids of sidewalk   Port Authority
thirty-fourth street Path Station

to Hoboken to the Erie-Lack-
awanna old green trains
like a Lionel set we once played with

     wicker seats flip direc-
tions make it hard to know what's coming
          what's going and
                    your sleep is coma's trial run
when the conductor once Virginian bass-baritones

        "Convent Station"
the words slap into a creviced shadow of sleep
knock you
        out of the train
you fall
      into a bevy of passing nuns

        "Sisters of Mercy"
who happen to know your mother
and don't take you to the state hospital

        "Greystone Park"
take you home   because this is a town
a while longer
      that you recognize

               and recognizes you.

At The Payne Whitney Clinic

Here is Miss K—in the fixed position of a wrought-iron S
  over the toilet, a frozen cry—*Help me decide*—a voice locked inside,
    a solid fecal log hangs just touching the bowl's still water.

Mrs. M disimpacts eleven Louis Vuitton suitcases, folds, unfolds
  twelve angora cardigan sets. Husband brings three more—
    cranberry, ochre, and opaline—he gifts her goodbye;

Mr. Mike, fly-swatting his back, a field where insects breed,
  centipedes eating millipedes, *God Save the Queen*, and poor Queenie,
    closet-locked for her first five years, follows him

picking up carcasses, tucks them under the rows of her braids.
  This is 1981, and Dr. L, that is me at twenty-nine,
    trying to make sense of this world.

Dr. L must conduct group therapy, gathers Mrs. M, Mike,
  Queenie, not K. Others come to show a healing wrist, a rope
    burn. The room should be quiet, fills with street-noise. What engine?

What is back-firing? Dr. L can't tell who is speaking, who not.
  His brother enters the room, but that's impossible. Two months ago,
    at twenty-two, he overdosed. The doctor can't remember

his brother's name. Is he there, someplace among the many pages
  of the roster? *The New York Times* on a breezy Sunday in Central Park,
    Help Wanted, flies to the top of an oak. He reaches into the air,

the group quiets, reaching with him. So many arms, hands like nets
  waving, slowly, synchronized. He must comfort them all.
    Everyone. Or maybe he has. He can't push past his lips the words

murmuring in his throat and wonders how ventriloquists sing.

The Net

The letters of your name in the air I reach for them with a net.
  Good thing for the silver fireflies drifting through the evening,
    I would have been thought mad. *Oh Dear Brother—*

old aunts are still bringing chocolates. I have swooped some up—
  some silver kisses. Uncle Lou has cracked his hip. I want to tell
    a story, say sorry, August dog days and all, you were wild,

I hooked you to the dog-run, barking at the afternoon and the kids,
  their laughter, now with the net's long pole can't collect, or soothe
    your face redder than sunburn. Silver letters from your name

escape the words I'd write—the night's evening is wide, and the net—
  I've got some of Grandmother's letters here and a luna moth
    tearing its wings flapping with blame—the net is getting full.

My cello's in there. Take it back, strings and bow. Dad's silver dollars
  spent on cigarettes and gum. Oh Dad, who couldn't cry, his sides
    cut and burst, slivered with a case of shingles rough as a fallen roof,

my arms so tired, the net so full, and Michael your friend cut himself
  with a silver knife. His blood inks the sky darker yet, the night's evening
    wide, the net so full, the more I swish the net, the more the moon fades.

How do I write when you hardly knew to read? A postman stalks
  this sky, this wide dark sky. Here, this satchel, this burgeoning net.
    Here, a letter of your name drifts into the vast night's evening

across acres of a flying cemetery, and the sky, a sky of migrating souls.
  Oh the dark night's evening, and my net is full of silver holes.

Where now

do our hands clasp?

Between gravel path and granite,
each reaching for the other,
no longer turn away, the warm

and cold of it (and Grandfather
turning his face toward the door,
the sun, the chill October breeze,
he closed his eyes, I did, too,
and eyes glowing red we talked
about making fall resolutions,
how many he had and I, none
back then, and in a soft laugh
said—as if I could have known
more; I remember that same
child swimming an August lake,
the sudden up-drift, a glacial spring
hitting me like a fist in the belly,)
I kept going, kept going . . .
that same man, the frozen
sadness returning, ice-leaching,
eyes unwilling . . .

between gravel path and granite
brothers breaching
the warm and cold of it

reaching out . . .

I place a pebble on his stone.

iv.

Owl Flight

For Susan: A Prologue

You ask—what are you thinking
. . . or perhaps you didn't ask.
I am not sure I heard

words through the dark
across the pillow-cleft, your lips
if speaking burned with light,

turned our bodies into
light, and lit the room,
now, like the after-image

of a quick-struck match
our thoughts without the sash
of words have settled

undeciphered on the bed—
I'm thinking of the day we met,
how that day becomes history,

a story within our past
as if we were once settlers
piling unearthed stones

to claim a field out of the acres
of a vast frontier. Here we build
and here we begin again.

I hang my past on the walls,
Mother, Father, Brother,
all have become ancestors

and I invite them to speak,
a word, a rustling of feet
along the floor, coax them

from the past to the present,
they, the key opening the future
for us, these ushers

wait, their pages of memoir
loose in the attic, memory itself
batting at the eaves.

A window in the wind
opens and shuts and opens again,
a wing's brush of wind,

the owl-flight—
who they are, who we've been, who
we become.

Please Finish the Conversation

Welcome to the House of Uninvited Guests.
Want to try to get their attention? Get a word in?
I'm awake most of the time when they leave me

bored-to-death. Try to sleep, come evening
all at once they're here. How many bells
did you hear? They're crowding the kitchen

around the little pot of tea. Kettle keeps whistling,
open honey jar a buzzing hive of conversation.
They never finish what they're saying in this house.

It gives me a headache. The wife who walked,
who let her in? And Mother instructing the mayor
on how he's supposed to remember Father.

I should have sat her down long ago,
gotten the whole story. How long could it take?
Eight hours? What's eight? What are these numbers?

Nurse! Green lines are jumping the overhead
screen. Who ever gets the whole story, beginning
to end? Give them all the lie-detector test!

"Oh yes, and it's so good to see you . . .

Urgency

A voice, an owl of desperation
I am still blocks away from,
and she cries that she is dying
and she is. My mother, her cousins,
a generation. Her cough hatchets
the dark I race through, the ambulance
blares ahead of me—*Oh friends!*
Not these sounds! I lose her, too.
It's dangerous to be alive and lonely.
Do you come crashing down, you millions?
And what of the newly painted ceiling,
buckling and cracking, what of the sky,
star-points swelling, bursting, extinguishing—

Summersong

I heard my father down the hall, his calls for help echoing,
I rushed across the years to my mother. I heard my father.

She cried: *I want my grandmothers here.* With me. Her night-
gown fell, she flung herself to bed, breasts bare and crying.

How mute my father, who found her, still mourning, longed
to find her and there, did nothing. How mute before

this, my mother into the demented years, long after
she had died, hair disheveled shocks, this my mother.

When I spoke she remembered her care, remembered
something deeply, as if a knife of fire when I spoke.

Where are the cicadas? I'm a biologist. I've waited seventeen long years.
All the years in one song. Like a grandmother. Where are the cicadas?

The stars fell from the sky, a copious fall, carcasses of light
on roofs, walls, mountains, down gutters of lava the stars fell.

With cicadas singing, the stars fell. I saw beyond the once
of dying, and birth, memory shed, singing again with cicadas.

A Bridge in Venice

Among church-named squares
and the gaze of their saints,

just after *Campo Santo Moïse*
heading towards the Academy—
is it *San Maurizio? Stefano?*—

coming up on a small bridge
my dead father.

Without breath I stop.
Can I reach him?

He is thinner,
glasses too large for his face,
his scapulae,
stunted limbs pushing
at the drape of his pale cotton shirt.

He has turned, taking the air.
He looks down a small canal
seeing the Adriatic beyond.
He has been to Venice only once,
decades before I lived here.

He manages the stairs well
a plastic cannula by his nose,
pulling an oxygen tank
the many widows around him
clattering their shopping carts.

Could I have heard the lumbering?

A white shadow
lays on his cheek. A hurried shave?
He has somewhere to go, these last
of his days, and these are the days

after his last. He carries
a bouquet of poppies,
too long a widower,
he has someone to meet.

Her laughter rises to all his jokes—
   *heard the one
   about the Litvak and the Galitzianer,
   heard the one . . .*

And he likes to bless each day
with a Latin quote—
   vox clamantis in deserto . . .
   vocem perdidit in solitudine . . .

She never questions the route
he insists on taking, sketched in a moment
from the many maps filed in his mind.
                  He was never lost.

I hear him humming a medley of tunes—
Verdi, Cole Porter, Gershwin.

I might have imagined the Verdi,
and don't stop him,

don't want him to be late.

New Year's Eve

Evening at the door
   my dead father comes in
as if he can cloak himself in the shadow of another
                           new year's guest,
their swarms of talk,
   and even before I see him, the musty smell of his coat.

He's taken again to visiting, regularly, I might add,
and I've told him just pretend to understand,
       float between
conversations, or be a shrink like me with meaningful
hmm's or *tell me more's*—but no, he's taken seven canapés.

Who can tell what hunger
   fills with this meat, this cheese, mustard and bread?
I thought his body fed
   on light   or sound.
      I am watching him chew.
I can't tell who sees him, who not, or how.

Now Mrs. Liebstraum angles closer, pretending
   she doesn't want that pinch on her ass
and I thought she had long ago given up on men,
at least earthly ones.
   What passes between his finger and thumb, anode

and cathode to what energy? An arm's length away,
she's already smiling a feline curl, and he's forgotten again
which world he's in. I wish he'd decide!
         I shake him by the lapels
and I'm seen swatting winter flies.

and my arms fill with real weight,
        a crumple, a spasm. It's his back,
gone out again, and he folds
onto the day bed, complaining that the leather
pillow-roll is too high! Always another ailment!

My face barometers his wincing.
How is one body beset by so many ills?—yet
                        I'm the doctor he wants.
His legs, sinuses, indigestion, enema tubes,
the swollen heart, the failing lungs—
A textbook of pathology, almost living,
        his look says—
Study me—
        another warns—
                        With Time—

He pulls out a pocket watch,
wants me to take his pulse.
His look also says I can't know yet
what he's done to give us another evening together.

My hands soften, like a pair of nurses,
bring him velvet, slip it under his stiff neck.
They ignore me when I say he'll be fine,
go on adjusting the cushion, seem to ask
                how pain carries on
still wanting solace.

It's as deep as my name in granite
here etched in his brow
    I try to wipe away but can't.
            With sweeps of confetti,
        eddies of streamers,

I hear the singing from the hallway

and hum to him,

auld   auld   auld

auld lang syne.

What Will Happen in the End

The owl skims the night river
like a single wing
   of the moon, and the river
comes carpeted

with ice and the owl rims
   the river of night, becomes
two wings, now four;
         the white wind

careens in cold; white wings
beat the rising wind, the rising
   waves break
     beyond the discernible

as if the wind
a phosphorescent flood
rushes from the seed
      of the owl's eye.

Art in Heaven

(Approaching Summer, the Jersey Shore)

Greetings!—for time present and time past
this is the country for old men, our Father, who
is still intrigued by the Zinfindels, explains how
the grape skin left in the barrel gives it a blush.
Mom removes her sunglasses, lifts her glass
of the clearest Pinot Grigio, toasts the long
June evening. An empty bottle of wine is
a microphone to the next world. A holler
into its small mouth—and leave a bit of hooch
at the bottom so they can wet their whistles, too.

Eternal time is dry, is filled with ethereal sounds,
silos-full, sifting, pouring through funnels
to earth. Leave the whistling to them, or call
the glistening out of the sky. The light
of hammered metal will swarm on wings
thinner than foil, than stretched cellophane,
and from the specks—the Byzantium birds!
Much has been made of golden artifice.
Each joint, pinioned and placed, makes its own
racket. How many wings beat that sky?

From the back porch we see Lucifer,
the neighbor's dog, tha-lump by . . . a dove
in his mouth. Now a dark flock of grackles
gather in the splendid oak, its branches
spreading from a single trunk, our tree,
and through its single, deep-piercing root, sap
rising from the molten center. All covet
this tree, the history written in its bark, its limbs
destined to be cut and crossed. Scattered across
the yard, other trees, a dozen yews on tripod roots

clutching the stony rubbish just under the lawn.
The silver wind-quiver of the leaves stirs a fear
of blasphemies. See the shadowed men seeking shade?
They murder in fear.
                  My singing-master cries—
Summer is a-comin' in! Mom takes a heart-shaped
welk from the porch's ledge, from the waves
of Long Beach Island. *Take a listen!* Even Dad
lets his ear peer in. He nods. *For time future!*
We all nod—the sound, so similar, so different.

The Map: You and I

in the noisy scatter of the "you's"
  and "I's," you've got to learn
    the sounds of their voices.

They're all around us with insect-buzz,
  bird-warble, prayer-growl, panting-laugh,
    and in my throat the teenage cracking

of boy and man and all the ways
  we celebrate birthdays of youthfulness.
    In the singing, can you hear the accents?

The whole family piles in, the rip in the screen
  an open invitation, even ones without names
    and some never leave. I don't want them to.

Sometimes you'll hear them in my voice,
  maybe before I will. They speak for me,
    right in the middle of my words, even make me

speak for them—like when I was packing up
  Mother's belongings, a gift, a never-worn
    lavender cardigan I was supposed to return,

and half way to the department store
  realizing it had closed ten years ago
    and still she insisted her friend would give us

credit. Get it? Ditto. I'm listening for you too
  and the many generations of you's
    that haven't finished their business.

This is the primer.
   The lexicon.
      The encyclopedia.

Such a strange species! Look us up.
   See how we mate.
      Love the strange,
                        and love the nest.

To My Firstborn

I hate to do it, but do it anyway.
  To set myself heavily beside you.
    To leave my bossy words.

I have just walked through
  the door you call home
    and I am telling you what is needed.

You'll tell me—would it really matter
  if the doorposts were marked?
    You'll say he cares for you, your lawyer

of right and wrong who drinks our wine,
  knows it by vintage and year,
    knows all but its blessing.

And I am telling you a dark shadow
  will enter the unmarked door. Is he strong
    enough to wrestle the intruder to the ground?

As if I believe in that angel of death,
  as if those angels could tell a firstborn
    from the others, as if a father stood by,

and yesterday, I passed the school bench
  where I once waited, the fruit stand
    where you'd pick only the hardest apples,

Delicious, Gala,
  slip notes into my pocket,
    joke of the day, wish of the day,

and gathering every note and letter,
   every page of homework I ever saw,
     I throw by the handful an offering

into the air the flock of white pigeons
   promising to circle your building
     day and night, just ahead of the wind's fetch.

Bouquet

The flowers, my son's gift—
he's never given me such thanks before.

Again he's leaving, wants to settle up.
This moment I'm like a stiff album opening,

how I try not to remember
(his mother,

he also brought her flowers, across town)
the bright scents, the mingling of hurts

my hand, half salt-water, half fresh
drawn across his face.

V.

First Waltz

You've given me a chance,

but I'm not going to take a chance.
Chance is not the partner I court.

(But when I did court chance
with wonder what it would

reveal, I wished chance were not
the certainty that . . .)

Love appears!

"Per quelli chi voliano"

(Installation, Fondation Maeght)

For those who fly, or those
who mean to fly . . .

a park bench on the museum roof,

patient in its angle of waiting,
a way-station for the air-born.

Jumping Dogs

(after the painting by Geoffrey Moss)

forever stretching
arcs of contrary leaping
over the pink and orange sofa

how in this painting
the drips tell
a story of imperfection

and those dogs
finding each other mid-air
like you and I

I Do

Not my father, not colleague, not mentor
        Dr. Williams (W. C.)
has been to the ballet
          and writes
    his own *Danse Russe.*

He struts in front of his mirror

      naked,

grotesquely, he says,
  and while his family sleeps
    declares himself:

happy genius of the household.

If he can, I can. I try it.
  Part chicken—I cluck.
    Part owl—there's stealth.

You there—belly and knobby knees—

        know what?
Go ahead and ask—

I would.
  I will.
    I do.

For a minute

knowing
the night breeze knocking
the shade against the window,

the minute passing through
the room and still twilight glowed
on your shoulder and hair,

there in this minute knowing
I need you beside me,
your hand tracing my arm

again your hand against my back
and there a heaven of dancing
minutes, the marks of minutes

blinking the way a clock counts
time, but dancing, linking,
weaving the lines of dancing,

and there a story, a blanket,
a comforter; there a breeze;
there breath made whole.

Water like Honey

Water like honey,
bread like meringue—

What has come over me?

All day, I'm holding your hand
or I'll float away.

Spring Rainsong

I like the rain my pants cuffed wet,
the late walk home, the bus stop near,
the wild pears with street light glow
are paving white the sidewalk pale.
Late the rain and light the trees,
in my shoes before the door—
the walk I haven't taken yet. Before
the door my shoes are wet, and soft
the rain before the door. And soft the fall.

Fire in the Piano Warehouse

It is singing.
As I always hoped
to make it sing.

The woods give back their resins
to light and song and the metal
harps return to their base elements
as if they themselves were composers.
The strings in high-note tension
ping back to their pure pitches.
The billows, the smoke, the firemen
ready their hoses but cannot douse
the inferno of this symphony
and the masters of the ghostly whirl
hold back the quenchers' hands
and fill intoxicated lungs—

They can barely say:
We have never seen a piano burn.
We have never seen a society
of pianos burning.

First Waltz

Invocation

It started a thousand years ago.
From this day, it goes on a thousand more.

We bring an in-gathering
of exiles, taken from themselves

scattered along the rivers of home.
They march in the sunrise. They whisper

the names of loss, waiting. We give
them back their lost voices.

We give them back their names
as they hear a new song.

Singing does not save them.
It can only make them worthy.

Teach us to listen.

Ceremony

When I first heard your voice,
the first call, a single note.

A foot on the sill, a boat at the dock—
teach me to listen.

In the gallery you stepped from a frame.
Now a lifetime.

We take flowers to the ship's bow
before rocks scrape away the paint's sheen,
before barnacles crust its smooth side.

Trumpets herald the launch, trombones
the lilt of oars.

We pull anchor when two links of pure gold

we put on each other's fingers and make a vow—
from Sinai, from Minsk, from Baghdad,

from across the pale of settlement
toward *die goldene medina*, we, utopia

with outstretched arms, boatloads
of the generations
held to living by our embrace.

This moment, we are history's magnet.
My name was on the invitation and it's changing!
Asher son of Simcha, son of Asher. Oscar!
Oscar who?

And you, Sarah, daughter of Israel
daughter of Fay, lighter than your veil.
Her father has arrived, the rabbi from Jerusalem.

The list unfurls like a scroll,
   everyone with a smile and nod.
A cadre of past lovers parade, clapping.
They are giving up their claims, take back
trinkets and watches, return libraries of lent books,

gallons of cologne whirling in the drain.

Now my patients, and some of your father's—
   deformed children zig-zagging
through the crowd, spinning tops of oddity.

A shoulder like a backpack, legs and arms swinging
at different lengths like tentacles. Eyes peering
on diagonal across face.

                They play kazoos, ukuleles,
crash cymbals, a kitchen mishap of falling plates.
They are singing their thank-yous.

Their laughter is the triangle's ping.
Their bodies today are whole.
I stoop to welcome them—they disappear!

Behind them—
   the children misused by adults.
They are Sinai's burning bush, burning,

never consumed. Their skin always hot,
eyes pulsing lanterns of light.
                    Only survivors

can see their flame, smell the smoke that hangs
in their quiet words. They bless us. Of the seven
blessings for bride and groom—they are the eighth.

It is a blessing of trust,
when trust, like the door of privacy, is smashed.

It's the song of the carpenter, piecing together
the splinters of wood, of the glazer mending
the shards,
    the roofer, shingle by shingle

putting back what the winds tore away.

We are all survivors, and more of our dead
    sail in. On the cello's bow, the oboe's breath.

They're hanging on the walls like pictures,
    lamp-auras, echoes of greeting, the spittle of a kiss.

What post office delivered their invitations?
What border stamped their visas of passage home?

We will greet everyone. Hold my hand.
My heart as loud as a schoolyard!
    And yours, your heart races the butterflies.

Celebration

We've been fasting for all the years before.
We eat and morsels fill. We dine
    on the minutes.

We sip with hummingbirds,
and for them the woodwork adorned
with hanging vines and flowers.

Sweetmeats and ginger, jewels
                dissolving in fountains
of wine. We serve currants, plums—and joy

and it's no longer ours alone.

The clarinet calls.
    Our pied piper is back from his dusty journey.
A clap of hands: Everyone! Up from the feasting!

Tap feet to the wedding march. Drink
    from the loving-cup, the clocks spin
faster than roulette wheels, some forwards,

some back, weather vanes whirling into the wind.
    The clocks like fireworks explode. Their arms
reach to the comets, their numbers fly with asteroids.

There's no alarm to this marching. No boots!
No click of heels! No goose-steps! No salutes!
    It's the Bobover Rebbe's Wedding March!

Give his scraggly beard a kiss! *Yamulkes*
like flying saucers. Confetti.

The down-beat, the up-beat moving—
here, there—the drummer drunk
                    on a swig of plum schnapps.

Even the elders fast-step the weaving line.

The clarinet

leads down the stairs into the dance hall,
greets an accordion like a lover, violin and bass.

   It's the *Ershter Vals*, the first
waltz and I promise you. Oh I promise you!

It's Krakau, 1901. New York, 2014.
Time winks tonight! Do not be afraid.

We make of time what we will.

Our will tonight is everyone's,
and the gates of time are open. The wish to see
is seeing—a husband in his first sweetness,
        the bride lets down her hair.

We are the floating ribbons across the floor.
How the crystal lights the room! Dance on!

In dem zal shendelir fun krishtol,
                    your gown glows brighter,
how the music is light, twisting with our steps,

we are inches off the floor, everyone sees it,
swears to it, by the golden

rings on our fingers, there are
   wings on our shoulders, the chandelier
as bright as the sun. *Sheynste keynign fun ershte bal,*

eternally beautiful queen of the first waltz!
   How the guests out run the music.

Come back! Dance on! Our dance, the lasso
   thrown into time. The music quickens,

catches, passes hand to hand, shoulder
   to shoulder, on the chairs we are champagne

corks bobbing on the dancing sea,
   the sea swells up, still higher
we are cloaked in the chandelier's mantle.

Our bodies rise into the chandeliers.
   No one will ever set them down, they fly

beyond the sunset beyond the lights. Its beams
   a yellow rain of weeping. The moonrise
beyond the sun. Our planet, our galaxy

embraces two moons and a veil of stars.
   We are waving good-bye, waving hello.

What have we done to each another, and what
   will we do? We will go, and we still stay.

We will remember the praise
   of splinters and shards. This wedding

      starts again, forever.

NOTES

p.2   Images of this poem reference various Chagall paintings. The *shetl* energy will return in the final sequences of the book in *First Waltz*.

p.19   A *gett* is a Jewish divorce. It is a formal procedure which is sequentially represented in this poem. A *Bet Din* is a rabbinic court. Unlike secular divorces, the gett does not seek to attribute blame but serves as an act of dissolution and release.

p.20   *Va-yeishev* is a chapter of Torah, Genesis 37, read in the week that this gett is taking place. The name derives from the first line of the chapter, "And he lived."

p.32   The *chuppah* is the Jewish wedding canopy.

p.36   This poem references the Jewish custom of leaving a small stone on a gravestone after visiting. The reference is repeated on p.46.

p.39   *Hey Jude*, the song performed by The Beatles, written by Paul McCartney. The Devereau School is a therapeutic school.

p.44   The Payne Whitney Clinic is a psychiatric hospital in New York City.

p.52   Italicized lines are quotes from Schiller's *Ode to Joy*, the lyrics of the chorus of Beethoven's 9th Symphony. The first quote is the familiar opening, "*O Freunde, nicht diese Töne!* Oh friends, not these sounds." The second, "*Ihr stürzt nieder, Millionen?*" loosely translated as, "Do you come crashing down, you millions?" and in Schiller's context, down on your knees in prayer.

p.55   Litvak and Galitzianer refer to speakers from areas with distinct dialects of Yiddish, often the source between them of jokes.

p.55 *Vox clamantis in deserto*—The voice that cries out in the wilderness. *Vocem perdidit in solitudine*—A voice lost in solitude.

p.57 "With time," references Giorgione's 1506 painting *The Old Woman,* who carries a small banner, "*Col tempo,*" a warning that the ravages of age come to all who live long enough.

p.60 *Art in Heaven* references the spiritual worlds of W. B. Yeats (*Sailing to Byzantium*) and T.S. Eliot (*The Four Quartets*), and obliquely, Ezra Pound (*Ancient Music*).

p.64 Marking the doorpost refers to the tradition of placing a mezuzah on the doorframe, which recalls the exodus from Egypt when the Jews were instructed to brush sacrificial blood above their doors so the angel of death would pass over.

p.72 The poems references W. C. Williams, "Danse Russe".

p.81 *Celebration* invokes traditional klezmer and dancing. *Ershter Vals,* or *First Waltz,* is often played at weddings. Quoting the Yiddish from the lyrics, "*In dem zal shendelir fun kristol*" is a phrase from the line, "How the crystal chandelier lit up the room," and "*Sheynste keynign fun ershte bal,*" translates as, "Most beautiful queen of the first ball."

p.83 The praise of splinters and shards references the Jewish tradition of the groom breaking a wine glass at the end of the ceremony, just before the celebration begins. Its meanings are many—at the time of joy, pain and destruction are remembered. In an alternate Kabalistic view, the universe is in shards (*shevarim*), and humans must strive to put these pieces together. The union of a couple symbolically brings the incomplete pieces of life together, but even at a time when life seems whole, one must remember the pieces.

ABOUT THE AUTHOR

 Owen Lewis, the recipient of the 2016 International Hippocrates Prize for Poetry and Medicine, is the author of *Best Man* (Winner of the Jean Pedrick Chapbook Prize, New England Poetry Club), *Sometimes Full of Daylight*, and *March in San Miguel.* He has received awards from *The Mississippi Review, Connecticut River Review,* Kent and Sussex Poetry Society (UK), London School of Jewish Studies (UK), Ver Poets (UK), and The Amherst Writers and Artists Press. He is a psychiatrist and professor at Columbia University where he teaches with the narrative medicine group.

BOOKS BY DOS MADRES PRESS

◖◗ 2004

Annie Finch - *Home Birth*
Norman Finkelstein - *An Assembly*
Richard Hague - *Burst, Poems Quickly*
Robert Murphy - *Not For You Alone*
Tyrone Williams - *Futures, Elections*

◖◗ 2005

Gerry Grubbs - *Still Life*
James Hogan - *Rue St. Jacques*
Peter O'Leary - *A Mystical Theology of the Limbic Fissure*
David Schloss - *Behind the Eyes*
Henry Weinfield - *The Tears of the Muses*

◖◗ 2006

Paul Bray - *Things Past and Things to Come*
Michael Heller - *A Look at the Door with the Hinges Off*
Michael Heller - *Earth and Cave*
Richard Luftig - *Off The Map*
J. Morris - *The Musician, Approaching Sleep*

◖◗ 2007

Joseph Donahue - *The Copper Scroll*
Pauletta Hansel - *First Person*
Burt Kimmelman - *There Are Words*
Robert Murphy - *Life in the Ordovician*
William Schickel - *What A Woman*

◖◗ 2008

Michael Autrey - *From The Genre Of Silence*
Paul Bray - *Terrible Woods*
Eric Hoffman - *Life At Braintree*
Henry Weinfield - *Without Mythologies*

❭2009

Jon Curley - *New Shadows*

Deborah Diemont - *Wanderer*

Norman Finkelstein - *Scribe*

Nathan Swartzendruber - *Opaque Projectionist*

Jean Syed - *Sonnets*

❭2010

Gerry Grubbs - *Girls in Bright Dresses Dancing*

Michael Henson - *The Tao of Longing & The Body Geographic*

Keith Holyoak - *My Minotaur*

Madeline Tiger - *The Atheist's Prayer*

Donald Wellman - *A North Atlantic Wall*

❭2011

Pauletta Hansel - *What I Did There*

Eric Hoffman - *The American Eye*

David M. Katz - *Claims of Home*

Burt Kimmelman - *The Way We Live*

Bea Opengart - *In The Land*

David A. Petreman - *Candlelight in Quintero-bilingual ed.*

Paul Pines - *Reflections in a Smoking Mirror*

Murray Shugars - *Songs My Mother Never Taught Me*

Madeline Tiger - *From the Viewing Stand*

James Tolan - *Red Walls*

Martin Willitts Jr. - *Secrets No One Must Talk About*

Tyrone Williams - *Adventures of Pi*

❭2012

Jennifer Arin - *Ways We Hold*

Jon Curley - *Angles of Incidents*

Sara Dailey - *Earlier Lives*

Richard Darabaner - *Plaint*

Deborah Diemont - *Diverting Angels*

Richard Hague - *During The Recent Extinctions*
R. Nemo Hill - *When Men Bow Down*
W. Nick Hill - *And We'd Understand Crows Laughing*
Keith Holyoak - *Foreigner*
Pamela L. Laskin - *Plagiarist*
Austin MacRae - *The Organ Builder*
Rick Mullin - *Soutine*
Pam O'Brien - *The Answer To Each Is The Same*
Lianne Spidel & Anne Loveland - *Pairings*
Henry Weinfield - *A Wandering Aramaean*
Donald Wellman - *The Cranberry Island Series*
Anne Whitehouse - *The Refrain*

▶2013

Mary Margaret Alvarado - *Hey Folly*
John Anson - *José-Maria de Heredia's Les Trophées*
Gerry Grubbs - *The Hive-a book we read for its honey*
Ruth D. Handel - *Tugboat Warrior*
Eric Hoffman - *By the Hours*
Nancy Kassell - *Text(isles)*
Sherry Kearns - *Deep Kiss*
Owen Lewis - *Sometimes Full of Daylight*
Mario Markus - *Chemical Poems-One For Each Element*
Rick Mullin - *Coelacanth*
Robert Murphy - *From Behind The Blind*
Paul Pines - *New Orleans Variations & Paris Ouroboros*
Murray Shugars - *Snakebit Kudzu*
Jason Shulman - *What does reward bring you but to bind you to Heaven like a slave?*
Olivia Stiffler - *Otherwise, we are safe*
Carole Stone - *Hurt, the Shadow-the Josephine Hopper poems*
Brian Volck - *Flesh Becomes Word*
Kip Zegers - *The Poet of Schools*

◗2014

John Anson - *Time Pieces - poems & translations*
Ann Cefola - *Face Painting in the Dark*
Grace Curtis - *The Shape of a Box*
Dennis Daly - *Nightwalking with Nathaniel-poems of Salem*
Karen George - *Swim Your Way Back*
Ralph La Charity - *Farewellia a la Aralee*
Patricia Monaghan - *Mary-A Life in Verse*
Rick Mullin - *Sonnets from the Voyage of the Beagle*
Fred Muratori - *A Civilization*
Paul Pines - *Fishing on the Pole Star*
Don Schofield - *In Lands Imagination Favors*
Daniel Shapiro - *The Red Handkerchief and other poems*
Maxine Silverman - *Palimpsest*
Lianne Spidel & Anne Loveland - *A Bird in the Hand*
Sarah White - *The Unknowing Muse*

◗2015

Stuart Bartow - *Einstein's Lawn*
Kevin Cutrer - *Lord's Own Anointed*
Richard Hague - *Where Drunk Men Go*
Ruth D. Handel - *No Border is Perennial*
Pauletta Hansel - *Tangle*
Eric Hoffman - *Forms of Life*
Roald Hoffmann - *Something That Belongs To You*
Keith Holyoak - *The Gospel According to Judas*
David M. Katz - *Stanzas on Oz*
Sherry Kearns - *The Magnificence of Ruin*
Marjorie Deiter Keyishian - *Ashes and All*
Jill Kelly Koren - *The Work of the Body*
Owen Lewis - *Best Man*
Paul Pines - *Message from the Memoirist*
Samantha Reiser - *Tomas Simon and Other Poems*

Quanita Roberson - *Soul Growing-Wisdom for thirteen year old boys from men around the world*

David Schloss - *Reports from Babylon and Beyond*

Eileen R. Tabios - *INVENT[ST]ORY Selected Catalog Poems and New 1996-2015*

Kip Zegers - *The Pond in Room 318*

❧2016

Anthology - *Realms of the Mothers-The First Decade of Dos Madres Press*

Eduardo Chirinos - *Still Life with Flies [naturaleza muerta con moscas]*, Bilingual, English translation by G. J. Racz

Norman Finkelstein - *The Ratio of Reason to Magic: New & Selected Poems*

Gerry Grubbs - *The Palace of Flowers*

Richard Hague - *Beasts, River, Drunk Men, Garden, Burst, & Light - Sequences & Long Poems*

R. Nemo Hill - *In No Man's Ear*

W. Nick Hill - *Blue Nocturne*

Nancy Kassell - *Be(longing)*

Rick Mullin - *Stignatz & the User of Vicenza*

Sharon Olinka - *Old Ballerina Club*

Bea Opengart - *Duties of the Heart, a Verse Memoir*

Michael Rothenberg - *Drawing the Shade*

Natalie Safir - *Eyewitness*

Daniel Shapiro - *Woman at the Cusp of Twilight*

Madeline Tiger - *In The Clearing*

John J. Trause - *Picture This: For Your Eyes and Ears*

Leonard Trawick - *A 24-Hour Cotillion*

John Tripoulas - *A Soul Inside Each Stone*

Panagiotis A. Tsonis - *An Autobiography*

Anne Whitehouse - *Meteor Shower*

Geoffrey Woolf - *Learn to Love Explosives*

David Almaleck Wolinsky - *The Crane is Flying - Early Poems*

Tyrone Williams - *Between Red & Green: Narrative of the Black Brigade*

www.dosmadres.com